SO-BNI-349

PRINCETON STUDIES IN INTERNATIONAL FINANCE

No. 77, February 1995

THE HECKSCHER-OHLIN MODEL IN THEORY AND PRACTICE

EDWARD E. LEAMER

INTERNATIONAL FINANCE SECTION

DEPARTMENT OF ECONOMICS
PRINCETON UNIVERSITY
PRINCETON, NEW JERSEY

INTERNATIONAL FINANCE SECTION
EDITORIAL STAFF

Peter B. Kenen, *Director*
Margaret B. Riccardi, *Editor*
Lillian Spais, *Editorial Aide*
Lalitha H. Chandra, *Subscriptions and Orders*

Library of Congress Cataloging-in-Publication Data

Leamer, Edward E.
  The Heckscher-Ohlin Model in theory and practice / Edward E. Leamer.
  p. cm. — (Princeton studies in international finance, ISSN 0081-8070 ; no. 77)
  Includes bibliographical references.
  ISBN 0-88165-249-0 (pbk.) : $11.00
  1. Heckscher-Ohlin principle. 2. Comparative advantage (International trade). I.
Title. II. Series.
HF1411.L423 1995
382—dc20
                                    94-49591
                                        CIP

Printed in the United States of America by Princeton University Printing Services at Princeton, New Jersey

International Standard Serial Number: 0081-8070
International Standard Book Number: 0-88165-249-0
Library of Congress Catalog Card Number: 94-49591

CONTENTS

FIGURES

TABLES

1 INTRODUCTION

According to the Heckscher-Ohlin factor-proportions theory of comparative advantage, international commerce compensates for the uneven geographic distribution of productive resources.[1] This is obvious in some respects but not so obvious in others. It is not a great theoretical triumph to identify conditions under which countries rich in petroleum reserves export crude oil, and it would not be a great surprise to find supportive evidence. But it is a theoretical triumph to find conditions under which countries that are richer in labor than land export labor-intensive agricultural products and, as a result of trade, have wages that approach levels prevailing in high-wage labor-scarce countries. And it would be a great surprise to find supportive data.

The basic insight of the Heckscher-Ohlin (HO) model is that traded commodities are really bundles of factors (land, labor, and capital). The exchange of commodities internationally is therefore indirect factor arbitrage, transferring the services of otherwise immobile factors of production from locations where these factors are abundant to locations where they are scarce. Under some circumstances, this indirect arbitrage can completely eliminate factor-price differences. Perhaps the most important implication of the HO model is that the option to sell factor services externally (through the exchange of commodities) transforms a local market for factor services into a global market. As a result, the derived demand for inputs becomes much more elastic, and also more similar across countries.

A feature that goes hand in hand with an elastic labor-demand function is an aggregate gross domestic product (GDP) with a relatively constant marginal productivity of capital. This is a critical property because growth induced by capital accumulation is generally limited by the declining marginal productivity of capital.[2] In an HO model of a

Able research assistance for this study was performed by Robert Murdock. Research support was provided by a National Science Foundation grant.

[1] Flam and Flanders offer an account of the model's intellectual history in their introduction to Heckscher and Ohlin (1991).

[2] Romer (1986) sparked a boomlet of sustainable-growth models that emphasize externalities but that depend critically on a constant or increasing long-run marginal productivity of capital.

1

small open economy, however, the potential decline in the marginal productivity of capital is completely offset by a shift in the product mix toward capital-intensive products. In a closed economy, by contrast, shifts in the product mix are necessarily more limited because everything has to be sold internally. Thus, growth is more easily sustained in open economies than in closed ones.

That's the theory. What about the facts? Is there any substantial evidence that international commerce compensates for the uneven geographical distribution of factors of production? If there is an association between trade and factor abundance, which is the direction of causation? What resources should be considered internationally immobile and over what period of time? Is the derived demand for labor actually more elastic in an open economy than a closed one? Is growth sustainable in open economies but not in closed ones?

Facts casually and not so casually collected seem to be adding up to a convincing case against the HO model. The first was Leontief's (1953) troubling discovery that U.S. imports in 1947 were more capital intensive than U.S. exports. For several decades, this blow to the HO model was thought to have knock-out power, but Leamer (1980) showed that it missed the mark because of a misreading of the theory. Bowen, Leamer, and Sveikauskus (1987) did not intend to attack the HO model but, although doing the correct calculation, found what seems to be a disappointingly small association across countries between factors embodied in trade and factor supplies.

Another set of troubling facts was provided by Grubel and Lloyd (1975), who cataloged the surprising amount of two-way trade in even finely disaggregated trade data. Furthermore, trade among the industrial countries has been growing much more rapidly than output, even as these countries have apparently become more similar in their factor endowments.

While these troubling facts have been accumulating, a formidable group of trade theorists led by Brander, Dixit, Grossman, Helpman, and Krugman have been crowding the HO model out of academic discourse by publishing a vast array of interesting models that focus on economies of scale and strategic interactions.

Yet the HO model remains very much alive and well, residing happily and prominently in every textbook on international economics written by authors fond of the artistic diagrams and simple, remarkable theorems associated with the HO viewpoint. Without saying so explicitly, these textbook writers remind us that theories are neither true nor false. Theories are sometimes useful and sometimes not so useful. These authors understand that data analysts may hit the HO model so hard that it hollers "false," and that theorists may pin the model so firmly to the mat that it squeals "impressed," but the authors have not heard, nor do they imagine ever to hear, the HO model scream "useless." In fact, the HO model is extraordinarily useful pedagogically, politically, and empirically.

Pedagogically, the model offers a loud wake-up call to the limitations of partial-equilibrium thinking. Does an increase in the supply of labor lead to a lower wage rate? "Of course," is the partial-equilibrium answer. "Not necessarily," is the HO answer, because trade allows the potential effect of an increase in the labor supply to be partly, and sometimes fully, offset by a shift of the product mix in favor of sectors that use labor intensively. The increased supply of labor-intensive products can be absorbed externally with little or no effect on product prices.

Politically, the HO model lends intellectual support to the warning "keep your crummy government mitts off international trade." This contrasts greatly with the appeal inspired by the modern trade theorists, "fight the decline of America; support an industrial policy before it's too late." According to the HO model, tariffs and quotas have redistributive effects but reduce efficiency. When redistribution is the legitimate goal, there is generally a better way to accomplish it. For example, Ross Perot's "social tariff" to offset the wage advantage of Mexico, Latin America, and Asia might help to maintain high wages for unskilled workers in the United States, but it would be a terribly costly way to achieve only modest changes in the U.S. income distribution. The "new" trade theorists may see the issue differently; they have bombarded us with models showing that the interest of the United States lies in "protecting" certain sectors, thereby encouraging production on a more efficient scale and also giving U.S. firms a strategic advantage over foreign rivals. These are thought-provoking but very dangerous ideas. Every trade barrier of which I am aware was really erected to redistribute income, not to capture unexploited economies of scale or strategic advantages. Rent-seeking lobbyists already have plenty of subtle and not-so-subtle ways to coerce Congress into supporting their redistributive agenda. When academics supply models that lend intellectual support to these schemes, lobbyists skillfully turn the remote possibilities suggested by the models into seeming certainties, and they thus turn unpalatable income transfers into compelling industrial policies.

Last but not least, the HO model is empirically useful because it helps us to understand important aspects of the patterns of international trade.

The rest of this study develops the idea that the HO factor-proportions model is useful in three ways: As a theory, as a description of reality, and as the key for understanding the impact of globalization on the U.S. labor market. The next chapter uses the familiar Lerner-Pearce diagram to derive some rather remarkable theoretical conclusions. These should have an indelible effect on your thinking, which of course is one of the key tests of the usefulness of a theory. Chapter 3 provides an algebraic treatment of the "even" model with equal numbers of factors and goods and with both home bias and neutral technological differences. Chapter 4 summarizes the recent history of international commerce with a graphical three-factor, multigood model. Chapter 5 supports these theoretical ideas with some empirical evidence. Chapter 6 deals with the hot topic of globalization and wages.

2   THE LERNER-PEARCE DIAGRAM IN ACTION

Some of the most interesting results obtainable from a Heckscher-Ohlin framework come from an extraordinarily simple figure, the Lerner-Pearce diagram. The diagram is routinely used to demonstrate the Factor-Price-Equalization Theorem and the Stolper-Samuelson Theorem, but it can be manipulated to produce a great variety of other interesting results.

Factor-Price-Equalization Theorems

Figure 1 displays two unit-value isoquants labeled machinery and apparel. These show combinations of capital and labor that can be used to produce a dollar's worth of output. The potential dependence of this figure on the choice of monetary unit ($1 or $1 million) is eliminated by the assumption of constant returns to scale. The dependence of the figure on the relative price of machinery to apparel is implicit, though this price

FIGURE 1

FACTOR-PRICE DETERMINATION IN A LERNER-PEARCE DIAGRAM

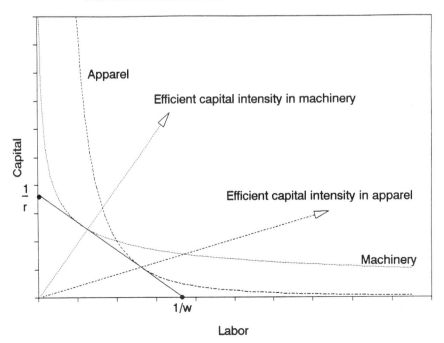

5

can be taken as given for many comparative-static exercises, because it is determined in the international marketplace.

In this figure, machinery is relatively capital intensive and apparel is relatively labor intensive. The solid line connecting the points labeled $1/r$ and $1/w$ is the only unit-isocost line compatible with the production of both of these products. Any other isocost line would either leave unexploited profit opportunities or would force a sector out of existence because of negative profits.

The equation for this isocost line is $\$1 = wL + rK$, where L and K are the amounts of labor and capital that are employed and w and r are the corresponding rental charges for these inputs. This equation can be solved for the two points where the isocost line crosses the axes, $1/w$ and $1/r$—hence the labeling in the figure. Perhaps without noticing it, you have now seen how to solve for the factor prices, w and r, given product prices and given technologies with constant returns to scale. No reference has been made to the country except that it produces both of the goods. To introduce a country into this figure, we need only identify the point representing the country's supplies of capital and labor. If full employment is assumed, the set of capital-to-labor factor-supply ratios compatible with the production of both goods is the interval between the capital-to-labor ratios in apparel and machinery. This set of factor supplies is called a "cone of diversification." In summary, we have established the following:

The Factor-Price-Insensitivity Theorem. For a small open economy, the derived demands for factors are infinitely elastic (within cones of diversification).

This may seem like an uncomfortable way of summarizing the logic that leads from product prices and technologies to factor prices, but it is actually the most accurate way of doing so. The traditional way of expressing the result is:

The Factor-Price-Equalization* Theorem. Countries producing the same mix of products with the same technologies and the same product prices must have the same factor prices.

Regrettably, this theorem is misleadingly labeled, for by using the word "equalization," it suggests a process rather than an outcome. To help make the correction, I have added the asterisk so that you can search and replace "equalization*" with "equality." It is the "Factor-Price-Equality Theorem," not the "Factor-Price-Equalization Theorem." Next is a result that does refer to a process, not just the outcome:

The Factor-Price-Convergence Theorem. When two countries eliminate their mutual trade barriers, product-price equalization eliminates factor-price differences.

Of these three results, the Factor-Price-Insensitivity Theorem requires the least restrictive assumptions, and it is the theorem that most closely fits one of our basic themes, that the option to sell commodities externally turns a local labor market into a global labor market. This option increases the elasticity of the derived demand for labor in this 2 by 2 model to infinity. The Factor-Price-Equalization° Theorem is a stronger result and requires additional assumptions: identical technologies, no factor-intensity reversals, and/or sufficiently similar factor-supply ratios. The Factor-Price-Convergence Theorem is different in subtle but important ways. First, by its lack of explicitness, it challenges us to find combinations of assumptions regarding factor-supply differences, technological differences, and numbers of factors and goods for which economic integration reduces international factor-price differences. Second, it makes explicit reference to the "signal" by which the effects of economic integration are transmitted among countries. This signal is the change in product prices resulting from integration—not, for example, an elimination of technological differences or a migration of factors or even an increased volume of international trade. Both the Factor-Price-Insensitivity Theorem and the Factor-Price-Equalization° Theorem take this price signal as fixed, so they fail to provide an intellectual setting in which factor-price convergence can be studied.

Factor-price convergence induced by product-price convergence can be studied with the aid of the Stolper-Samuelson Theorem, which links factor prices with product prices. It is also easy to use the Lerner-Pearce diagram to establish:

The Stolper-Samuelson Theorem. An increase in the price of the labor-intensive product causes an increase in the real-wage rate and a reduction in the real return to capital.

To prove this result, simply shift the apparel isoquant inward toward the origin to reflect the fact that, at a higher price for apparel, less capital and labor are needed to produce a dollar's worth of output. This shift is accompanied by a twisting of the unit-isocost line, reflecting a reduction in $1/w$ and an increase in $1/r$.

7

Applications of the Lerner-Pearce Diagram

The Lerner-Pearce diagram has an extraordinary number of interesting applications. Several are presented below. I shall list the result and refer to the corresponding figure but leave readers pretty much on their own to connect the two.[1]

High wages come from product upgrading. A country will have high wages if it is sufficiently abundant in capital to concentrate production on capital-intensive products and exchange these on world markets for labor-intensive products.

This possibility is depicted in Figure 2, which shows three products, machinery, textiles, and apparel, and two countries, the United States and China. The United States has high wages and produces machinery and textiles. China has low wages and produces textiles and apparel.

The United States and China are only partly integrated in Figure 2, and the remaining differences in factor costs create incentives for labor to flow from China to the United States and for capital to flow from the United States to China. In reality, we see both labor flows and capital flows. The integration of East and West Germany seems to be inducing much more rapid labor flows than capital flows. In the U.S.-Japanese case, by contrast, capital has been the factor bringing about a fully integrated equilibrium, not by a capital outflow from the United States, but by much higher saving and investment rates in Japan. Incidentally, factor movements in search of higher returns will change the worldwide supplies of products and induce product-price changes that tend to "melt" away the differences between the cones.

High wages come from high demand for nontraded goods. Communities can have high wages for unskilled workers if they concentrate production on capital-intensive tradeables and absorb unskilled workers, partly to produce these skill-intensive products and partly to produce labor-intensive nontradeables.

Figure 3 illustrates this possibility with two traded goods, machinery and apparel, and one labor-intensive nontraded good, services. Two possible equilibria are depicted, one with low wages and apparel

---

[1] The isoquants in these figures are all right-angled and thus use capital-to-labor ratios that do not vary with factor prices. This assumption of fixed input technologies reduces the clutter in the graphs without altering the basic results. The first several results are standard textbook material. The latter ones are, I believe, new.

FIGURE 2
TWO-CONE LERNER-PEARCE DIAGRAM

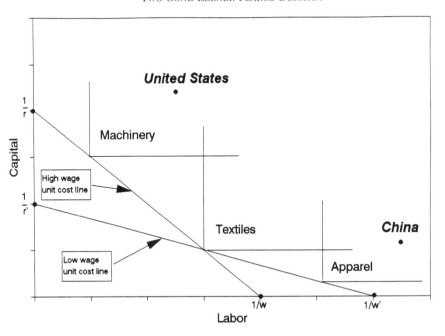

FIGURE 3
HIGH-WAGE AND LOW-WAGE EQUILIBRIA WITH A NONTRADED SECTOR

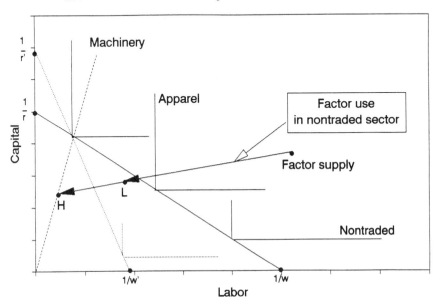

production, the other with high wages and no apparel production. These differ in terms of the amounts of factors absorbed by the nontraded sector. The low-wage solution leaves the amount L for production of tradeables, and the high-wage solution leaves the amount H. The low-wage solution seems to have been adopted by Los Angeles, which has an active apparel industry. The city of Seattle may illustrate the high-wage solution, with tradeables output in aerospace and computer software.

Minimum wages raise wages even in uncovered sectors.[2] A minimum wage with an uncovered labor-intensive tradeables sector lowers the return on capital and raises wages in all sectors, but by more in the covered sectors than the uncovered sectors. It does not cause unemployment.

Figure 4 illustrates a case in which there are four products, a covered capital-intensive tradeables sector, an uncovered labor-intensive tradeables sector, and both a covered and an uncovered labor-intensive nontradeables sector. Think of the covered tradeable as aerospace and

FIGURE 4

EFFECTS OF A MINIMUM WAGE WITH ONE UNCOVERED TRADEABLE SECTOR

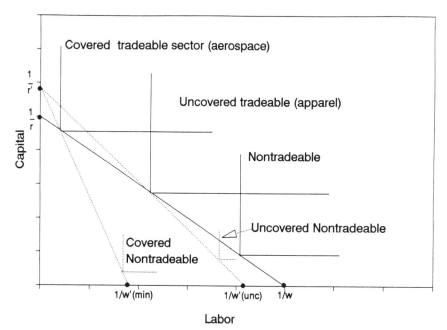

<hr>

[2] Carruth and Oswald (1982) give the algebra of the two-sector model with one covered and one uncovered sector.

the uncovered tradeable as apparel that is produced in small shops, where it is difficult to enforce the minimum wage. Think of the covered nontradeable as McDonald's and the uncovered nontradeable as housekeeping. According to this theory, wages in the uncovered garment district in Los Angeles are raised by minimum wages in the covered aerospace industry. The higher wages must then be paid by employers in the nontradeable sector, the costs of which are passed on to consumers in the form of higher prices.

Talented workers receive a wage premium only in capital abundant countries. Workers with God-given talent will receive the same earnings as untalented workers if they are employed for the same tasks. If the capital-intensive sector makes use of the talent, but the labor-intensive sector does not, then capital-scarce countries will have talented workers working alongside untalented workers in the labor-intensive sector, and both kinds of workers will receive the same low wages. Capital accumulation expands the talent-using capital-intensive sector, which eventually gets large enough to employ all the talented workers, who then enjoy a wage premium over the untalented workers. Thus, income inequality increases with capital accumulation.

Figures 5 and 6 illustrate two equilibria with a labor-intensive farming sector that does not distinguish talented from untalented workers and a capital-intensive "music" sector in which the talented workers are more productive than the untalented workers. In Figure 5, capital is too scarce to allow all of the talented workers to be employed producing music. Some of the talented workers are employed on farms, and they thus receive the same low wages as untalented workers. In Figure 6, there is enough capital to allow all the talented workers to be employed producing music. The untalented workers also produce music, but they command a lower wage because they are less productive. (Note, incidentally, that the wages of the talented workers rise if the untalented workers become more productive in farming.)

If, however, the talent-using sector were labor-intensive, then capital accumulation would lower, not raise, income inequality. Based on this observation, let me throw out a half-baked idea that contrasts the industrial revolution of the nineteenth century with the information revolution of the twentieth century by focusing on the capital intensity of the sector that uses the talent. The technological innovations of the industrial revolution created mills and factories in which humans were indistinguishable inputs. Talent remained important in the labor-intensive

11

FIGURE 5

CAPITAL-SCARCE EQUILIBRIUM WITH TALENTED WORKERS ON FARMS

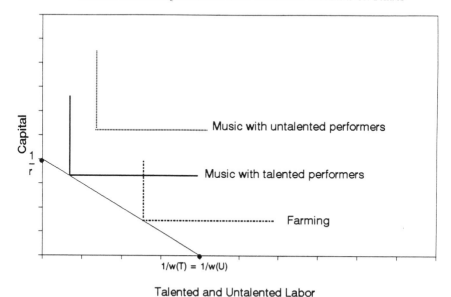

FIGURE 6

CAPITAL-ABUNDANT EQUILIBRIUM WITH TALENTED WORKERS NOT ON FARMS

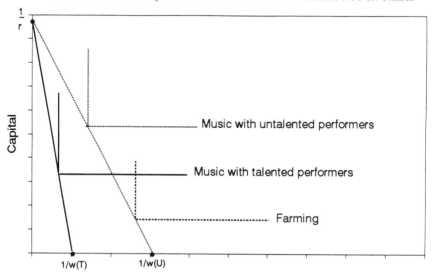

sectors, but capital accumulation pulled workers increasingly into the capital-intensive factory system, where they received higher wages but no compensation for talent. I think something very different is happening today. The revolution in information processing and communication is creating capital-intensive sectors in which the design and use of hardware and software require talent.[3] This threatens to make the twenty-first century a time of increasing income inequality in the capital-abundant countries.

Nonproprietary technological change can lower wages. Technological change in the capital-intensive sector lowers the real-wage rate when it is not accompanied by offsetting price changes.

Figure 7 has a unit-value isoquant for textiles and two different unit-value isoquants for machinery. The solid isoquant applies before the technological change, and the dotted one, requiring the use of smaller amounts of capital and labor, applies after the technological change.

FIGURE 7

TECHNOLOGICAL CHANGE IN THE CAPITAL-INTENSIVE SECTOR

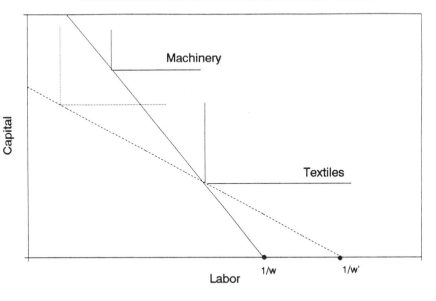

---

[3] Krueger (1993) finds that workers who use computers earn a 10 to 15 percent wage premium. This estimate accounts for one-third to one-half of the increase in the rate of return to education, but the calculation is not driven by a general-equilibrium model.

The computer revolution seems like a good example of relatively rapid technological improvement in the capital-intensive sector, but it has been accompanied by an extraordinary decline in computer prices. Such a price reduction in the capital-intensive sector would shift outward the unit-value isoquant for machinery and thus raise the wage rate, offsetting partly or even completely the initial downward effect on wages.

Technological change in the nontraded-goods sector has a rather different effect, because factor prices may be determined entirely in the traded sector. For example, suppose that the computer revolution reduces labor requirements in the nontraded labor-intensive service sectors. Think of automatic teller machines, answering machines, computer-aided design. Workers who are technologically displaced can continue to be employed in the nontraded service sector only if price reductions in that sector are large enough to generate an offsetting increase in demand. It is more likely, however, that these released workers will be employed partly in the traded sector. The increased supply of workers to the traded sector forces a shift in the output mix toward labor-intensive goods, and it will lower wages if the change in the output mix is substantial enough.

Capital can migrate to escape an inferior technology. A superior technology in the United States attracts equity investments from Mexico. In Mexico, this capital outflow has a redistributive effect in favor of capital and an overall efficiency effect, the latter but not the former depending on the amount of the capital flow.

In Figure 8, the heavy dotted line represents the final Mexican isocost line, with a rate of return to capital equal to that in the United States, but with a wage rate (w'_{MEX}) that is low enough to offset the higher capital costs in the labor-intensive sector. The amount of capital that exits Mexico is just enough to leave behind a capital-to-labor ratio that is suited to the labor-intensive sector. (If the isoquant were curved, the lower Mexican wage rate would dictate a more labor-intensive technique in Mexico than in the United States.)

Foreign direct investment transfers technology. Multinationals that raise capital in the United States and transfer technology to Mexico cause a redistributive effect in favor of labor in Mexico and an efficiency effect. The Mexican economy bifurcates, with the labor-intensive sector operated by U.S. multinationals using advanced technology and the capital-intensive sector employing Mexican capital and using backward technology.

FIGURE 8

CAPITAL FLOW FROM A TECHNOLOGICALLY BACKWARD COUNTRY

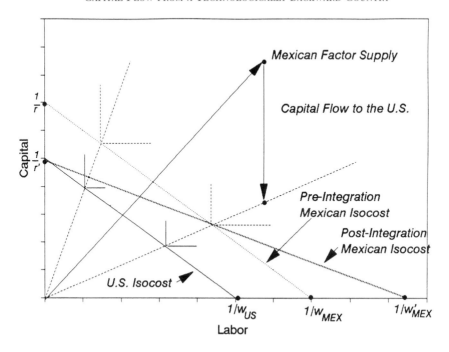

FIGURE 9

FOREIGN DIRECT INVESTMENT INTO A TECHNOLOGICALLY BACKWARD COUNTRY

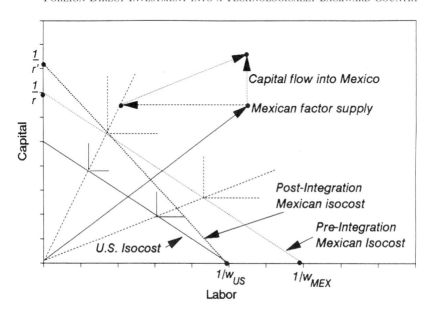

In Figure 9, the heavy dotted line represents the new Mexican isocost line, with a wage rate equal to that in the United States but a return to capital that is low enough to offset the higher labor costs in the capital-intensive sector. The U.S. multinationals transfer capital into the Mexican labor-intensive sector and hire labor locally. Just enough workers are employed by the multinationals to leave Mexican firms with a capital-to-labor ratio that is perfectly suited to the capital-intensive sector.

Figures 8 and 9 thus depict two very different kinds of partial integration between an advanced country and a backward one. Capital may flow out of the backward country into equities in the advanced country, leaving behind a labor force with a lower wage rate. Alternatively, capital may flow from the advanced country into the backward one, bringing with it an improved technology and increasing the demand for labor in the backward country.

3 ALGEBRA OF THE (EVEN) HECKSCHER-OHLIN-VANEK MODEL

Many results of an HO model can be derived and communicated most effectively with graphs, but the more precise language of algebra is useful for making assumptions clear and for introducing into the model both home bias and technological differences.

An elegant algebraic version of the HO general-equilibrium model is based on the assumptions of (1) identical homothetic tastes, (2) constant returns to scale and identical technologies, (3) perfect competition in the goods and factor markets, (4) costless international exchange of commodities, (5) factors of production that are completely immobile across international borders but that can move costlessly among industries within a country, (6) equal numbers of goods and factors, and (7) sufficient similarities in factor endowments to place all countries in the same cone of diversification.

The production side of the HO model deals with the mapping of prices (p) and resource supplies (v) into factor prices (w) and the output mix (q): $w = f(p,v)$; $q = g(p,v)$. Four theorems characterize the derivatives of these functions:

The Factor-Price-Equalization* Theorem	$\partial w/\partial v = 0$
The Stolper-Samuelson Theorem	$\partial w/\partial p \neq 0$
The Rybczynski Theorem	$\partial q/\partial v \neq 0$
The Samuelson Duality Theorem	$\partial w/\partial p = (\partial q/\partial v)'$

With equal numbers of goods and factors, the production side of the model can be summarized by the system of equations

$$q = A^{-1}v , \tag{1}$$

$$w = A'^{-1}p , \tag{2}$$

$$A = A(w,t) , \tag{3}$$

where q is the vector of outputs, A is the input-output matrix, with each element representing the amount of each factor used to produce a unit of each good, v is the vector of factor supplies, w is the vector of factor returns, p is the vector of commodity prices, and t is time. Equation (1), which translates factor supplies (v) into outputs (q), is the inverted form of the factor-market equilibrium condition equating the supplies of factors (v) to the demands for factors (Aq). Equation (2), which translates product prices into factor prices, is the inverted form of the zero-profit conditions equating product prices (p) to production costs ($A'w$). Equation (3) expresses the dependence of input intensities on factor prices (w) and on the state of technology, with $A(w,t)$ being the cost-minimizing choice of input intensities using the technologies available at time t. The assumption of constant returns to scale implies that A depends on the factor returns (w) but not on the scale of output (q).

The consumption side of the model is neutralized by the assumption of identical homothetic tastes. In the absence of barriers to trade, all individuals face the same commodity prices, and they consume goods in the same proportions:

$$c = s\,c_w = s\,A^{-1}v_w \,, \tag{4}$$

where c is the consumption vector, s is the consumption share, c_w is the world consumption vector, and v_w is the vector of world resource supplies. Thus, the vector of trade flows is

$$T = q - c = A^{-1}v - s\,A^{-1}v_w = A^{-1}(v - s\,v_w) \,. \tag{5}$$

The consumption share (s) will depend on the level of output and also on the size of the trade balance ($B = p'T$), where p is the vector of prices. Premultiplying (5) by the vector of prices and then rearranging, we obtain the consumption share:

$$s = (p'A^{-1}v - B)/p'A^{-1}v_w = (GNP - B)/GNP_w \,. \tag{6}$$

This is often called the Heckscher-Ohlin-Vanek model because of Vanek's (1968) use of the assumption of homothetic tastes. In this HOV model, trade is a linear function of the endowments. The more basic HO model makes no reference to linearity and merely concludes that trade arises because of the unequal distribution of resources across countries, with no trade occurring if the ratios of resources are the same in all countries.

A very informative way of writing (5) is $AT = v - s\,v_w$, that is, the factors embodied in trade (AT) equal the excess factor supplies ($v - s\,v_w$). This algebraic expression emphasizes the fact that international trade is really about the exchange of factor services; commodities are only bundles of factor services.[1]

---

[1] Incidentally, this algebraic form requires only identical matrices A for different countries, not equal numbers of factors and commodities.

Neutral Technological Differences and Home Bias

Countries that opt for economic isolation tend to fall behind technologically, the more so the longer the isolation persists. The former Communist countries are obvious examples. Indeed, it has been argued that the Communist command-and-control economy would have been much longer lived had global technology not advanced so dramatically in the second half of the twentieth century. The fundamental failure of the Communist system was its inability to keep pace with or assimilate the technological improvements that occurred at a dizzying rate in the West.

We clearly need to amend the HO assumption of identical technologies if we intend to pool data for the Western industrial economies with those of Eastern Europe, or for that matter with those of Latin America, China, India, and others that have adopted policies of separation.

It is also necessary to introduce home bias of some form. Gravity models have been used for several decades to demonstrate the clear effect of distance on trade. Yet we continue to build international trade models that make the schizophrenic assumption that countries are both infinitely far apart and infinitely close, the former assumption applying to factor flows and the latter to goods flows. In fact, the costs of doing commerce over long distances have two important effects on trade patterns. Countries that are geographically large have lower ratios of trade to GDP because they have much economic mass that is relatively far from an external border. Countries that are distant from major marketplaces are forced to depend more on home production and to specialize in those traded commodities that travel well over long distances.

Both technological differences and home bias are now introduced in a way that leads to a remarkably convenient and intuitively appealing conclusion, that is, home bias and technological differences have the same effect, reducing a country's trade proportionately in all categories. It is easy to correct for this shrinkage effect by dividing net exports of each product by a measure of total trade. The HO framework can then be used to explain the composition of trade, although not the total amount of trade.

Neutral technological differences among countries can be fairly easily added to the HO model. The production side with technological differences takes the form

$$q_i = A^{-1} v_i \delta_i \ ,$$

where q_i is the vector of outputs, A is the input-output matrix, v_i is the vector of measured resource supplies, and $v_i\delta_i$ is the vector of effective resource supplies after adjusting for technological differences (δ_i).

Trefler (1993) has suggested one form of home bias that is particularly easy to employ. Write the consumption vector as a weighted sum of the world-production vector and the home-production vector:

$$c_i = \alpha_i q_w + \gamma_i q_i \ ,$$

where q_w is the vector of world output. The usual HOV assumptions of homothetic tastes and identical prices imply that consumption vectors for different countries are proportional to each other, that is $\gamma_i = 0$. In this formulation, home bias has the effect of pushing the composition of consumption toward the home-production basket (q_i). Although this formulation is wonderfully convenient for modeling purposes, it is not obvious how to justify this form of home bias in terms of transport costs, production functions, and utility functions. Furthermore, the formulation does not adjust for the endogeneity of the home output mix (q_i), which should be more similar to the world's output vector for countries that are geographically large or far from major markets. These concerns notwithstanding, we may plow ahead.

Because trade is the difference between production and consumption,

$$T_i = q_i - c_i = q_i - (\alpha_i q_w + \gamma_i q_i) \ .$$

Defining the trade surplus as $B_i = p'T_i$, where p is the vector of prices, we can solve for α_i from $B_i = p'q_i - \alpha_i p'q_w - \gamma_i p'q_i$. Thus,

$$\alpha_i = [(1 - \gamma_i)GNP_i - B_i]/GNP_w \ ,$$

and

$$T_i = (1 - \gamma_i)q_i - \alpha_i q_w = (1 - \gamma_i)(q_i - q_w GNP_i/GNP_w) + B_i q_w/GNP_w \ .$$

Abstracting now from trade imbalances, so that $B_i = 0$, this becomes

$$T_i = (1 - \gamma_i)(A^{-1}v_i\delta_i - q_w p'A^{-1}v_i\delta_i/GNP_w)$$
$$= (1 - \gamma_i)\delta_i(A^{-1}v_i - q_w p'A^{-1}v_i/GNP_w) = (1 - \gamma_i)\delta_i\theta v_i \ , \qquad (7)$$

where $\theta = (A^{-1} - q_w p'A^{-1}/GNP_w)$. Although the world output vector q_w/GNP_w and the world price level (p) depend on the set of technology multipliers (δ_i), these do not vary across countries, and the matrix θ accordingly has no i subscript.

If there were no home bias $(\gamma_i = 0)$ and no technological differences $(\delta_i = 0)$, then (7) would become $T_i = \theta v_i$, which lacks only the scalar multiplier $(1 - \gamma_i)\delta_i$, affecting each element of the trade vector by the same proportion. Thus, home bias and neutral technological differences have the same effect: they alter the amount of trade but not its composition.

There are two ways that one might adjust empirically for these effects. One can estimate the full system of equations, treating $(1 - \gamma_i)\delta_i$ as a set of uncertain parameters. Alternatively, one can eliminate these effects by dividing the data by total trade:

$$Tot_i = \sum_j |T_{ij}| = (1 - \gamma_i)\,\delta_i \sum_j (|\{\theta v_i\}_j|) \ .$$

When T_i is divided by this measure of total trade, we obtain

$$T_i/Tot_i = \theta v_i / \sum_j (|\{\theta v_i\}_j|) \ , \tag{8}$$

a trade-intensity variable that depends only on resource ratios. The principal difference between this and the usual HOV model (Equation [5]) is that this function is nonlinear.

4 LEAMER TRIANGLES

The algebra in the preceding chapter works very well for the even model with equal numbers of factors and goods, but the graphics suggested in Leamer (1987) may be clearer for discussing the uneven model. Now that Jones and Marjit (1991) have done so, it does not seem too impolite to refer to the triangular arrays used for presenting the three-factor model as "Leamer triangles," though Sarah Simplex[1] would probably see it differently.

The three-factor model illustrated in Figure 10 has one commodity that uses human capital as an input (chemicals), three commodities that use only capital and labor (apparel, textiles, and machinery), and one commodity that uses only labor (handicrafts). This set is designed to capture essential features of the postwar economic histories of the United States, Europe, Japan, and the emerging countries of Asia. The model addresses two questions: What impact did capital accumulation in Europe and Asia have on the United States and by what economic signal are the effects communicated? The answers are that changes in the quantity and composition of output in Europe and Asia induced worldwide changes in relative product prices. These price changes affected the U.S. terms of trade and also altered the compensation paid to U.S. factors of production.

In the initial equilibrium depicted in Figure 10, the United States finds itself in the high-wage cone suited to the production of a highly capital-intensive mix of products: textiles, chemicals, and machinery. Germany and Japan are in the moderate-wage cone producing apparel, textiles, and chemicals. Asia (other than Japan) is very poorly endowed in capital and finds itself in the low-wage cone producing mostly apparel and handicrafts. The United States has a strong comparative advantage in machinery, but it imports chemicals from Germany, apparel and textiles from Japan, and apparel from Asia.

The arrows from the factor-supply points depict hypothetical changes in factor supplies. The United States, although enjoying an initial advantage from the uniqueness of its endowment, finds itself crowded over time by Japan on the one side and by Germany on the other side. In the meantime, capital accumulation takes Asia into the moderate-

---

[1] The standard linear-programing name for this triangle is a simplex.

FIGURE 10

GROWTH PATHS IN A THREE-FACTOR MODEL

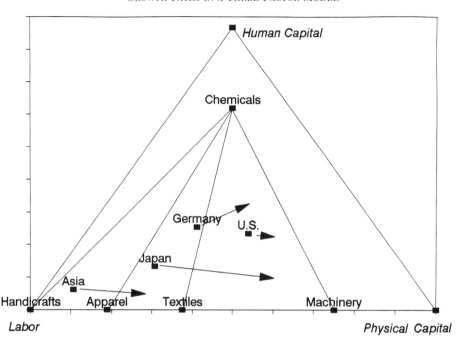

wage cone. The crowding around the United States, as well as the emergence of Asia, have implications for the U.S. terms of trade and for the returns to skill and physical capital. Because the United States is exporting machinery and importing textiles, chemicals, and apparel, a lowering of the machinery price represents a deterioration in its terms of trade, whereas a lowering of any of the other prices represents an improvement.

Changes in product prices also affect the wage level and the returns to human and physical capital. Table 1 reports the response of factor rewards to changes in the prices of the three U.S. products. The table also includes the effect on the skill premium, defined as the ratio of the return to human capital to the wage of raw labor. Loosely speaking, a commodity price and a factor price are positively connected if the factor is "suited" to the production of the commodity. One can determine if a factor is "suited" to the production of textiles in the following way (see Leamer, 1987, for a more complete explanation). Extend the line in Figure 10 connecting the chemicals point with the machinery point. If a factor input (say, labor) is on the same side of this line as

TABLE 1

EFFECTS OF PRICE CHANGES ON U.S. FACTOR EARNINGS

Reduction in Price of	Effect on U.S. Earnings			
	Raw labor	Human Capital	Physical Capital	Skill Premium
Machinery	+	+	−	?
Chemicals	0	−	0	−
Textiles	−	+	+	+

the textile point, then the factor and the commodity are "friends" (in Ethier's [1984] terminology); an increase in the price of textiles will raise the return to the factor. The opposite is true for factors with vertices on the other side of the line. As the figure is drawn, textiles are a friend of labor in the U.S. cone but an enemy of both human and physical capital; a rise in the price of textiles increases the wage of raw labor and lowers the returns to both physical and human capital. Things are rather different in the Japanese cone. Extend the line segment connecting the apparel point and the chemicals point to discover that textiles are an "enemy" of labor and human capital in the Japanese cone, and a friend of physical capital.

Conclusions regarding the effect of product-price changes on factor returns depend substantially and subtly on the input intensities. For example, if the machinery point is swung to the left, to a capital-to-labor ratio less than that of chemicals, then human capital and textiles become friends in the capital-abundant countries. A similar phenomenon affects the relative return to human capital in the U.S. cone compared with the Japanese cone. The Japanese cone in Figure 10 is relatively abundant in human capital, for there are paths from the U.S. cone to the Japanese cone directly toward the human-capital vertex. For that reason, the rate of return to human capital is lower in Japan than in the United States. This is the case even though the United States has an abundance of human capital and exports products intensive in human capital (chemicals). But the opposite ordering of the rates of return to human capital in Japan and the United States would occur if textiles had a higher ratio than chemicals of physical capital to labor.

Effects on the United States of Physical-Capital Accumulation in Japan

The initial accumulation of physical capital in Japan raises Japanese output of textiles and reduces Japanese output of apparel, but it does not alter Japanese production of chemicals. This is a result of the (implicit) assumption that input coefficients are fixed and that human capital is used exclusively in the production of chemicals. Thus, the output of chemicals is entirely determined by the supply of human capital, and the accumulation of physical capital alone shifts the mix of products from apparel to textiles, and then to machinery.

If Japan is a large enough country, the increased supply of Japanese textiles must produce an offsetting reduction in the price. This textile-price reduction increases the gap in wages between skilled and unskilled labor (the skill premium) in capital-abundant countries like the United States because it lowers the real return to unskilled labor and raises the return to human capital. Countries like Japan, in the moderate-wage cone, experience an increase in both the wage of raw labor and the return to human capital, and their skill premium can go either up or down.

Once Japan enters the high-wage cone, its output of textiles begins to decline and its output of machinery increases. A concomitant fall in the price of machinery lowers the return to physical capital but increases the return to both human capital and the wage of raw labor. Competition from Japan is thus likely to cause a deterioration in the U.S. terms of trade but to have an ambiguous effect on the skill premium.

Effects on the United States of Capital Accumulation in Germany

Initially, an accumulation of both human and physical capital in Germany reduces the German supply of apparel and raises the supplies of both chemicals and textiles. When Germany enters the high-wage cone, further capital accumulation reduces the supply of textiles and raises the supplies of both chemicals and machinery. A concomitant fall in the price of chemicals reduces the skill premium by lowering the return to human capital without changing the wage of raw labor. A fall in the price of machinery raises the return to both human capital and raw labor and therefore has an ambiguous effect on the skill premium.

5 EVIDENCE

The two preceding chapters were intended to dazzle you with theoretical insights derived from an HO framework. If they were successful, they will have changed fundamentally your views about unemployment, income inequality, direct investment, and global competition, without offering a single piece of evidence. This chapter will complete the seduction by demonstrating the empirical accuracy of the HO model. After that, we can move on to the main point of all this: public policy toward international trade.

Demonstration of the accuracy of the HO model requires a clear linkage of trade patterns with factor proportions. The first step is to select some sensible level of commodity aggregation, because the raw trade data are hopelessly detailed. Leamer (1984) invests a substantial amount of energy creating the ten commodity aggregates listed in Table 2. These aggregates were formed from observed correlations across countries of net export levels for more finely detailed product groups. For example, countries that export a large amount of cork and wood also tend to export pulp and paper. These are accordingly combined into a forest-products aggregate.[1]

This aggregation scheme has two raw-materials aggregates (petroleum and raw materials), four crops (forest products, animal products, tropical agriculture products, and cereals), and four manufactures (labor-intensive manufactures [LAB], capital-intensive manufactures [CAP], machinery [MACH], and chemicals [CHEM]). In terms of input intensities, the four manufactured aggregates are ordered by intensities in physical capital, but chemicals are generally more intensive in human capital than is machinery. These four manufactured products form a ladder of development that many countries have climbed, beginning with exports of apparel (LAB), moving on to textiles and iron and steel (CAP), and then to machinery (MACH) and chemicals (CHEM).

Patterns of Four Countries

Net exports per worker of these ten aggregates in 1958, 1965, 1974, and 1988 for Sweden, West Germany, the United States, and Japan are

---

[1] The Leamer (1984) study covered 1958 and 1974. Song (1993) extended the study and data set to 1988.

TABLE 2
COMPONENTS OF TEN COMMODITY AGGREGATES

Aggregates	SITC	Aggregates	SITC
Petroleum (PETRO)		**Cereals, etc. (CER)**	
Petroleum and derivatives	33	Cereals	4
		Feeds	8
		Miscellaneous	9
		Tobacco	12
		Oil seeds	22
		Textile fibers	26
		Animal oil & fat	41
		Fixed vegetable oils	42
Raw materials (MAT)		**Labor-intensive (LAB)**	
Crude fertilizers & minerals	27	Nonmetal minerals	66
Metalliferous ores	28	Furniture	82
Coal, coke	32	Travel goods, handbags	83
Gas, natural & manufactured	34	Art apparel	84
Electrical current	35	Footwear	85
Nonferrous metal	68	Misc. manufactured articles	89
		Postal packaging, not classified	91
		Special transactions, not classified	93
		Coins (nongold)	96
Forest products (FOR)		**Capital-intensive (CAP)**	
Lumber, wood, & cork	24	Leather	61
Pulp & waste paper	25	Rubber	62
Cork and wood manufactures	63	Textile yarn, fabric	65
Paper	64	Iron & steel	67
		Manufactured metal n.e.s.	69
		Sanitary fixtures & fittings	81
Tropical agriculture (TROP)		**Machinery (MACH)**	
Vegetables	5	Power generating	71
Sugar	6	Specialized	72
Coffee	7	Metalworking	73
Beverages	11	General industrial	74
Crude rubber	23	Office & data-processing	75
		Telecommunications & sound	76
		Electrical	77
		Road vehicles	78
		Other transportation vehicles	79
		Prof. & scientific instruments	87
		Photographic apparatus	88
		Firearms & ammunition	95
Animal Products (ANL)		**Chemicals (CHEM)**	
Live animals	0	Organic	51
Meat	1	Inorganic	52
Dairy products	2	Dyeing & tanning	53
Fish	3	Medical, pharmaceutical products	54
Hides, skins	21	Essences & perfumes	55
Crude animals & vegetables	29	Fertilizers	56
Processed animal & veg. oils	43	Explosives & pyrotechnics	57
Animal products n.e.s.	94	Artificial resins & plastics	58
		Chemical materials n.e.s.	59

illustrated in Figures 11 to 14.[2] The scales are the same in 1958 and 1965 but are larger in 1974 and larger still in 1988. These data conform rather well with the three-factor Heckscher-Ohlin history described in the previous chapter. In 1958, the United States is not particularly trade dependent, and it exports the full range of manufactured products, especially machinery. Germany has already emerged from the war, exports the full range of manufactured products, and imports all the crops and raw materials. Japan does not participate significantly in international trade but has a comparative advantage in manufactures that are lower on the development ladder (LAB and CAP).

The Swedish trade pattern in 1958 is particularly interesting because net exports are completely concentrated on forest products. Net exports of forest products amounting to $200 per worker paid for a mixed bag of imports including, especially, petroleum, tropical agricultural products, labor-intensive manufactures, and chemicals. To understand the pattern of Swedish trade, we need to include softwood forest resources as one of the factors of production. These softwood resources cause a "Dutch disease" for Sweden, namely, limited industrialization because of natural-resource abundance. Incidentally, the United States has an analogous comparative advantage in cereals.

There was a substantial increase in the amount of trade from 1958 to 1965. Both Germany and the United States climbed the ladder of development, becoming net importers of labor-intensive manufactures, and the United States also became a net importer of capital-intensive manufactures. Japan was emerging as a major global competitor in manufactures, concentrating low on the ladder of development by exporting labor-intensive manufactures but not chemicals. Swedish forest-product exports increased from $200 to $300 per worker, and the machinery sector was just beginning to emerge.

The emergence of the machinery sector in Swedish net exports is very pronounced by 1974, and the big increase in the price of petroleum is evident in all four countries, which show greatly increased petroleum imports. Sweden paid its petroleum bill with greatly increased exports of forest products and machinery. Indeed, one might suspect that the higher petroleum bill was the cause of the increase in net exports of machinery—a case of Dutch disease in reverse. Otherwise, the 1974 picture is very similar to the 1965 picture, although Japan is starting to give up on labor-intensive manufactures.

---

[2] Be alert that these are sectoral trade numbers divided by economywide labor-supply numbers.

FIGURE 11

NET EXPORTS PER WORKER, 1958

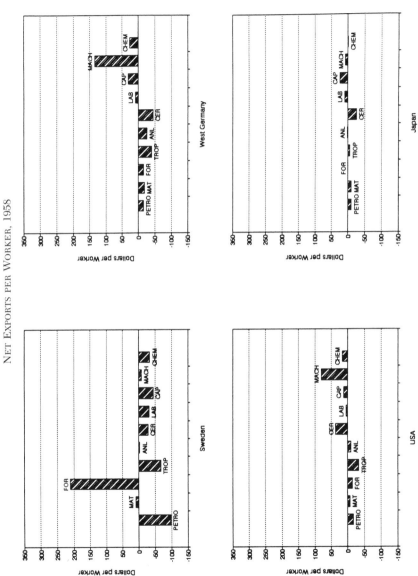

FIGURE 12

NET EXPORTS PER WORKER, 1965

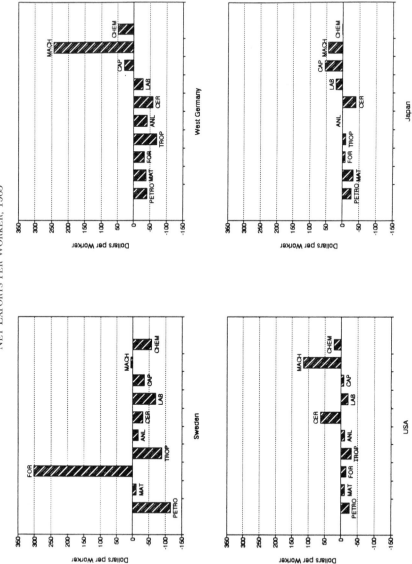

FIGURE 13

NET EXPORTS PER WORKER, 1974

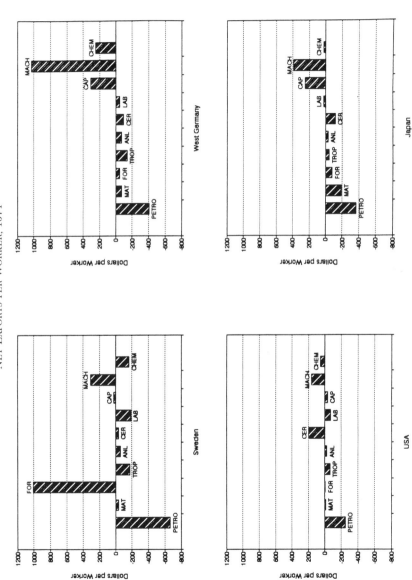

FIGURE 14
NET EXPORTS PER WORKER, 1988

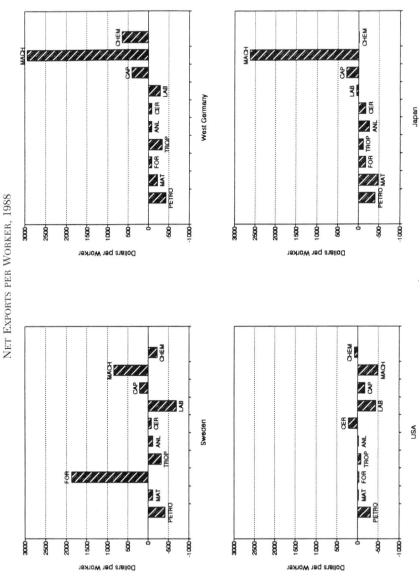

From 1974 to 1988, both German and Japanese exports of machinery increased enormously, apparently pushing Sweden half a step backward into greater reliance on net exports of capital-intensive manufactures, principally iron and steel. The United States is heavily affected by this competition and ends up looking like an agrarian society but with enough human capital to support a very modestly successful chemicals sector. Unless the trade deficit apparent in this graph is offset by net exports of services, the U.S. pattern in 1988 seems unsustainable, and we should expect a correction, probably in the machinery category.

Patterns over Time

The trade patterns of these four countries have been rather stable over time, and the changes that have occurred seem compatible with the idea that high investment rates in Asia are crowding the United States and Europe out of labor-intensive manufactures and into the most skill-intensive and capital-intensive products. To explore this idea more completely, Figures 15a and b and 16a and b report the full set of net export data for forest products and for labor-intensive manufactures, comparing 1965 with 1988. A full view and a zoomed view of each scatter are provided.

If there were no change in comparative advantage from 1965 to 1988, these data would all lie on a straight line. The forest-product data in Figures 15a and b conform relatively well to this straight-line norm, with only a few countries in the second and fourth quadrant. The big net exporters of forest products in both years were Finland, Sweden, and Canada. Norway experienced the most substantial change, switching from being a large net exporter to a large net importer. The stability of the trade in forest products is evident even in the zoomed view (Figure 15b), which displays only the smaller net exporters. Whatever the source of comparative advantage in forest products, it is not changing much over time.

By contrast, comparative advantage in labor-intensive manufactures (apparel and footwear), displayed in Figures 16a and b, is very much in turmoil, with a large number of countries shifting from being net importers to being net exporters, a feature that is particularly apparent in the zoomed view (Figure 16b). In response, France, the United Kingdom, Austria, and even Hong Kong have shifted in the opposite direction. Japan and Belgium, although still having positive net exports of this category, have substantially reduced their export dependence on labor-intensive manufactures, falling from among the top ten net exporters to well back in the pack. Moving in the same direction, net

FIGURE 15a

NET EXPORTS OF FOREST PRODUCTS PER WORKER, 1965 AND 1988

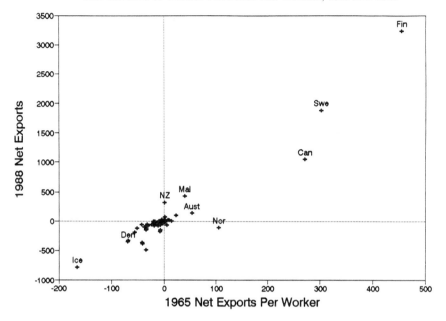

FIGURE 15b

NET EXPORTS OF FOREST PRODUCTS PER WORKER, 1965 AND 1988 (ZOOMED VIEW)

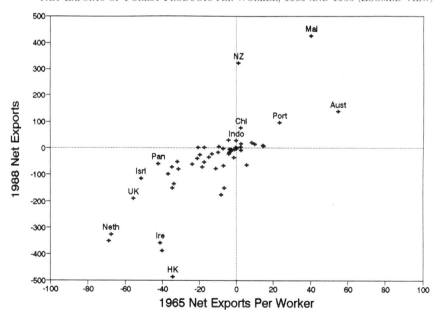

FIGURE 16a

NET EXPORTS OF LABOR-INTENSIVE MANUFACTURES PER WORKER, 1965 AND 1988

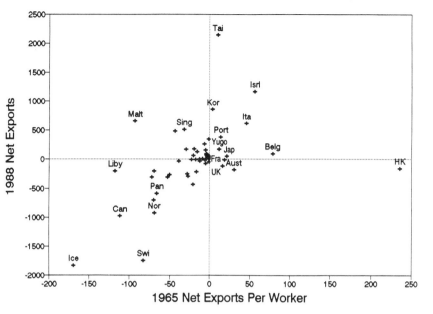

FIGURE 16b

NET EXPORTS OF LABOR-INTENSIVE MANUFACTURES PER WORKER, 1965 AND 1988
(ZOOMED VIEW)

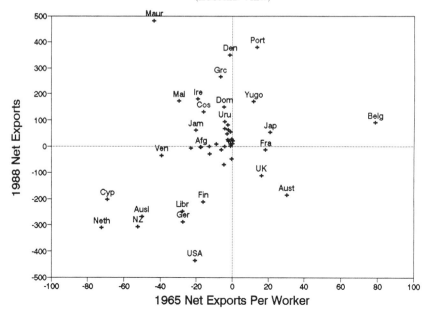

imports per worker by the United States increased by a factor of twenty-five over this period.

The other product aggregates (not displayed) have a degree of permanence in comparative advantage that is closer to the forest-product pattern than the labor-intensive pattern. The news in these scatters is thus stability, with one notable exception: crowding of the markets for labor-intensive products. This is exactly what would be predicted by the multicone HO model illustrated by the triangular Figure 10, which shows Asian countries taking over the markets for apparel, and Japan, Germany, and the United States shifting toward the more capital-intensive products.

Trade Patterns and Resource Supplies

Next, we need to link these trade patterns explicitly with factor supplies. Leamer (1984) argues that the patterns are adequately explained by the availability of eleven resources: capital, professional labor (Labor 1), literate labor (Labor 2), illiterate labor (Labor 3), tropical land (Land 1), arid land (Land 2), mesothermal land (Land 3), microthermal land (Land 4), minerals, coal output, and crude oil outputs. Song (1993) updates these results, without making major changes in the conclusions. Here I want merely to provide enough of the data's flavor to show that a factor-proportions model is helpful in understanding international trade.

Table 3 reports the largest simple correlations between net exports of each of the ten commodity aggregates in 1988 and factor supplies per worker. Correlations are reported with the trade data divided, first, by the labor force and, second, by total trade, the latter allowing for home bias and technological differences as discussed in Chapter 3. Two of the columns refer to "vetted correlations" in which two outliers (Egypt and Panama) are excluded. This very incomplete treatment of outliers will remind the reader of the large effect that one or two countries can have on these correlations.[3]

These simple correlations should be viewed as only a warm-up for the theoretically sound multidimensional analysis done in Leamer (1984) and Song (1993). For our limited purposes, these simple correlations are

---

[3] Omitting Egypt and Panama has little effect on the correlation with net exports per worker because the ratios of trade to work force are small for both countries. The vetting has a larger effect on several commodity aggregates when net exports are divided by total trade because both Egypt and Panama have very large levels of imports of these aggregates compared with total trade.

TABLE 3

LARGEST CORRELATIONS BETWEEN NET EXPORTS AND FACTOR SUPPLIES
PER WORKER IN 1988

	Net Exports per Worker			Net Exports/Total Trade		
Aggregate	Resource	Correlation	Vetted Correlation[a]	Resource	Correlation	Vetted Correlation[a]
Petro	Oil	0.65	0.65	Oil	0.35	0.37
Mat	Oil	0.54	0.54	Minerals	0.59	0.59
For	Land 4	0.45	0.45	Land 4	0.34	0.37
Trop	Capital	−0.52	−0.52	Capital	−0.47	−0.52
Anl	Land 3	0.27	0.27	Land 3	0.29	0.31
Cer	Land 3	0.51	0.51	Land 3	0.37	0.41
Lab	Capital	−0.42	−0.45	Land 4| Capital[b]	−0.29	−0.44
Cap	Capital	−0.15	−0.15	Capital	0.28	0.24
Mach	Land 3	−0.22	−0.24	Capital	0.22	0.42
Chem	Labor 1	0.14	0.14	Capital	0.47	0.60

[a] Egypt and Panama are outliers and are excluded.
[b] Vetting replaces Land 4 with Capital as the most important resource for labor-intensive manufactures.

enough. They show that trade patterns in many of these product aggregates are sensibly and closely linked with factor supplies, that net exports per worker of manufactures are difficult to explain with measures of factor supplies, but that net exports of machinery and chemicals divided by total trade are much better explained with factor supplies, particularly after vetting. This finding suggests that home bias and/or technological differences may be confined to the most capital-intensive manufactures.

These correlations will be accurate summaries of the data if the associations are linear and homoscedastic, which we can check by looking at scatter diagrams. Figure 17, which compares net exports per worker of labor-intensive manufactures with capital per worker, is one of the more interesting scatters. Nonlinearities here seem strongly present, with net exports per worker of labor-intensive manufactures not taking off until the capital-to-worker ratio reaches about $5,000, and then peaking at around $15,000 per worker. A piece-wise linear curve has been inserted into this scatter, and it is exactly the kind of development path that a two-factor multicone model would predict. The effect of natural resources on trade in manufactures can also be seen in this diagram, for some of the biggest importers are countries

FIGURE 17

NET EXPORTS OF LABOR-INTENSIVE MANUFACTURES PER WORKER
VERSUS CAPITAL PER WORKER, 1988

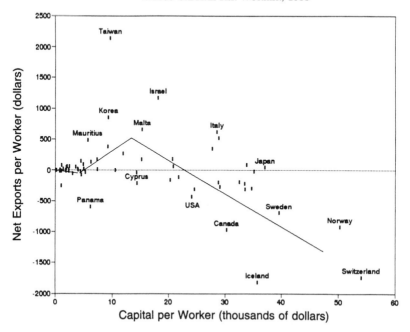

with abundant softwood forests (Canada, Sweden, and Norway). The figure also alerts us to the difficulties in cross-country comparisons, because we have here a measured capital-per-worker level for the United States that is substantially below the measured capital per worker for many other countries. Low savings and relatively rapid labor-force growth in the United States are real contributing factors, but proper adjustment for an overvalued dollar may also be important.

6 THE HECKSCHER-OHLIN MODEL AND INCOME INEQUALITY

The HO model seems like a pleasant and rather innocuous house guest, but it comes with two inseparable and somewhat troublesome traveling companions, the Stolper-Samuelson Theorem and the Factor-Price-Insensitivity Theorem. These two propositions link changes in income inequality to global commodity shocks and to migration, and they lead to dramatic conclusions about the possible consequences of the economic liberalizations that are sweeping the globe. These liberalizations have added to the global marketplace countries that have vast supplies of labor but very little capital. If the HO model is correct and international trade compensates for the unequal geographic distribution of factors, these liberalizations should be accompanied by a great burst in trade. If the Stolper-Samuelson Theorem is correct and if these liberalizations reduce relative prices of labor-intensive products in world markets, there may be large reductions in the earnings of those low-skilled American workers who are economically indistinguishable from Chinese or Mexican workers.

This is a very alarming possibility. Look at Figure 18, which shows the global labor pool in 1989. Each country is represented by a line segment with a width equal to its population and a height equal to its industrial wage. If the height were average labor earnings and the width were the labor force, then the area under a line segment would equal total labor earnings, which would be proportional to GDP if labor shares did not differ much across countries. Although these are only very rough approximations, the area under each line segment nonetheless gives a fairly accurate indication of the country's relative economic size.

In this figure, countries are sorted by wage levels. At the left are the high-wage countries. At the right are the populous but very low-wage countries. This creates a very unusual "pool" with the liquid piled up high at one end and hardly present at the other. What is holding up the high end? The HO model offers three possible answers: trade barriers, human-capital differences, and product-mix differences. Another possibility, which is straightforwardly introduced into an HO model, is the existence of technological differences.

According to the one-cone HO model, labor-abundant countries that opt for isolationist policies have low wages because they shut off the

FIGURE 18

THE GLOBAL LABOR POOL, 1989

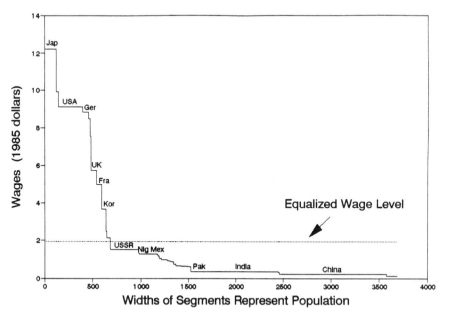

Widths of Segments Represent Population

arbitrage opportunity of exporting labor services at relatively high prices through the exchange of commodities. The removal of the trade barriers brings, first, product-price equalization and, then, wage equalization. If global labor earnings were held constant, the equalized wage level in Figure 18 would only be about $2 an hour, a heck of a lot lower than the U.S. level of $9.

There are two reasons why a fall from $9 to $2 is not predicted by the one-cone HO model. First, economic integration of the low-wage and the high-wage countries should be accompanied by worldwide gains from specialization according to comparative advantage, which raises total world GDP and probably raises global labor earnings as well. Second, the high wages in the United States and other high-wage countries are partly a return to (human) capital. Factor-price equalization in the one-cone model implies equal rewards for raw labor and for capital, but not for workers endowed with different levels of human capital.[1]

---

[1] Krueger (1968) offers estimates of the part of the cross-country variation in wages that is due to variation in skills.

40

Although the one-cone HO model does not imply that average wages in the United States must fall to the Chinese level, it does imply that U.S. workers who are economically indistinguishable from Chinese workers will receive the same compensation in an integrated equilibrium. This portends an alarming increase in income inequality in the United States as a consequence of the recent liberalizations. This dreary implication of the one-cone HO model, however, is not replicated by the multicone model. A multicone HO model allows the capital-abundant high-wage countries to protect even their lowest-skilled workers from the pressure for wage equalization if there is enough capital to support a capital-intensive mix of outputs, a possibility that was discussed above in Chapter 2.

Yet another more hopeful interpretation of the vast wage differences in Figure 18 is that they are due to technological differences. Economic liberalization can raise wages in the low-wage countries through technological transfers without having any impact on wages in the high-wage, technologically advanced countries.

This linkage of globalization with wage levels is not an idle academic exercise. The recent large increase in income inequality in the United States has precipitated an extensive search for the cause. The three big contenders are an increased supply of unskilled workers (educational failures and immigration), technological changes that are replacing humans with robots (computers), and globalization (lower prices for labor-intensive products, less market power in autos and steel, and increased international mobility of physical capital and technology). Measuring the effects of these forces is no easy task, and no one yet knows the exact contribution of each to the increase in income inequality. Clearly the task of estimating the effect of globalization on wages requires a theoretical framework, and the HO model is sure to receive renewed interest as a possible theoretical foundation for the study of this issue.

Three Mistaken Notions

It is not surprising to find labor economists doing data analyses without reference to the HO model, but substantial conceptual misunderstandings also appear in published discussions by prominent trade economists.[2] Three mistaken notions are:

---

[2] Estimates of the impact of "globalization" on U.S. wages are discussed in Freeman and Katz (1991), Lawrence and Slaughter (1993), Leamer (1993), Krugman and Lawrence (1994), and Wood (1994a, 1994b).

(1) The HO model depends on the substitutability of inputs within sectors.

Correction: The Factor-Price-Insensitivity Theorem, the Stolper-Samuelson Theorem, and the Heckscher-Ohlin Theorem do not depend at all on substitution between inputs within sectors. These theorems apply even if input ratios are technologically fixed. The Factor-Price-Insensitivity Theorem and the Heckscher-Ohlin Theorem are driven fundamentally by changes in the mix of products. The Stolper-Samuelson Theorem derives from zero-profit conditions that, when differentiated, leave input ratios unchanged.

(2) Globalization should be studied in the context of the Factor-Price-Equalization° Theorem.

Correction: The traditional Factor-Price-Equalization° Theorem is the wrong choice for studying the impact of increased foreign competition on the U.S. economy. Chapter 2 pointed out that the theorem is named in a highly misleading way, for the word "equalization" suggests a process by which wages are equalized by international commerce. Although the theorem identifies conditions under which two countries must have the same factor prices, it says nothing directly about the effect of increased external competition. Quite the contrary, it is based explicitly on the small-country assumption that external product prices can be taken as fixed even as the internal supply of product is varying. The Stolper-Samuelson Theorem, not the Factor-Price-Equalization° Theorem, is the correct choice for studying the effect of increased external competition on wages.

(3) External shocks are transmitted to internal labor markets by changes in the quantities of imports or exports.

Correction: According to the traditional one-cone HO model, shocks are transmitted to internal labor markets only by price changes, not by quantity changes. The Stolper-Samuelson Theorem indicates how wages change as international prices change. The Factor-Price-Insensitivity Theorem indicates that quantity changes do not matter, basically because the derived demand for labor is infinitely elastic.[3]

---

[3] Motivated informally by the central idea of the HO model that commodities are just bundles of factors, labor economists have calculated the factor content of U.S. trade and find that the net exports of labor services form a fairly small proportion of the U.S. labor force, only –0.25 percent (Bowen, Leamer, and Sveikauskus, 1987). Labor economists draw the conclusion that globalization cannot have had an important effect on income

In conclusion, then, the HO model continues to provide surprising insights. Not only is it useful as a theory. It accurately explains many prominent features of the patterns of international trade, and it is an essential ingredient in any study of the impact of globalization on the U.S. work force.

---

inequality. But this conclusion is a non sequitur if the HO model is used as a guide. The factor content of trade is determined by one set of equations (factor-market equilibrium conditions); factor prices are determined by another set of equations (zero-profit conditions). Indeed, the very essence of the Factor-Price-Insensitivity Theorem is that vast changes in the factors embodied in trade leave completely unchanged the compensation that these factors command. Factors embodied in trade can change because of internal factor-supply changes or because of changes in the demand for foreign products (including a trade deficit). Provided these changes do not alter the prices of the goods that are produced by the economy in question, there will be no change in factor prices.

REFERENCES

Bowen, Harry P., Edward E. Leamer, and Leo Sveikauskus, "A Multi-Country Multi-Factor Test of the Factor Abundance Theory," *American Economic Review*, 77 (December 1987), pp. 791-809.

Carruth, Alan A., and Andrew J. Oswald, "The Determination of Union and Non-Union Wage Rates," *European Economic Review*, 16 (June 1982), pp. 285-302.

Ethier, Wilfred J., "Higher Dimensional Issues in Trade Theory," in Ronald W. Jones and Peter B. Kenen, eds., *Handbook of International Economics*, Vol. 1, Amsterdam and New York, North-Holland, Elsevier 1984, pp. 131-184.

Freeman, Richard B., and Lawrence Katz, "Industrial Wage and Employment Determination in an Open Economy," in John M. Abowd and Richard B. Freeman, eds., *Immigration, Trade, and the Labor Market*, Chicago, University of Chicago Press, 1991, pp. 235-260.

Grubel, Herbert G., and Peter J. Lloyd, *Intra-Industry Trade: The Theory and Measurement of International Trade in Differentiated Products*, New York, Macmillan, 1975.

Heckscher, Eli F., and Bertil Ohlin, *Heckscher-Ohlin Trade Theory*, translated, edited, and introduced by Harry Flam and M. June Flanders, Cambridge, Mass., MIT Press, 1991.

Jones, Ronald W., and Sugata Marjit, "The Stolper-Samuelson Theorem, the Leamer Triangle, and the Produced Mobile Factor Structure," in Akira Takayama, Michihiro Ohyama, and Hiroshi Ohta, eds., *Trade, Policy, and International Adjustments*, New York and San Diego, Academic Press, 1991, pp. 95-107.

Krueger, Alan B., "How Computers Have Changed the Wage Structure: Evidence from Microdata, 1984-1989," *Quarterly Journal of Economics*, 108 (February 1993), pp. 33-60.

Krueger, Anne O., "Factor Endowments and Per Capita Income Differences among Countries," *Economic Journal*, 78 (September 1968), pp. 641-659.

Krugman, Paul, and Robert Z. Lawrence, "Trade, Jobs and Wages," *Scientific American*, 270 (April 1994), pp. 44-49.

Lawrence, Robert Z., and Matthew J. Slaughter, "Trade and US Wages: Great Sucking Sound or Small Hiccup?" *Brookings Papers on Economic Activity*, No. 2 (1993), pp. 161-226.

Leamer, Edward E., "The Leontief Paradox, Reconsidered," *Journal of Political Economy*, 88 (June 1980), pp. 495-503.

———, *Sources of International Comparative Advantage: Theory and Evidence*, Cambridge, Mass., MIT Press, 1984.

———, "Paths of Development in the Three-Factor *N*-Good General Equilibrium Model," *Journal of Political Economy*, 95 (October 1987), pp. 961-999.

———, "Wage Effects of a U.S.-Mexican Free Trade Agreement," in Peter M. Garber, ed., *The Mexico-U.S. Free Trade Agreement*, Cambridge, Mass., MIT Press, 1993, pp. 57-125.

———, *Sturdy Econometrics: Selected Essays of Edward E. Leamer*, Economists of the Twentieth Century, Aldershot, Hants, and Brookfield, Vt., Edward Elgar, 1994.

Leontief, Wassily W., "Domestic Production and Foreign Trade: The American Capital Position Re-examined," *Proceedings of the American Philosophical Society*, 97 (September 1953), pp. 332-349.

Romer, Paul, "Increasing Returns and Long-Run Growth," *Journal of Political Economy*, 94 (October 1986), pp. 1002-1037.

Song, Ligang, "Sources of International Comparative Advantage: Further Evidence," Ph.D. diss., Australian National University, 1993.

Trefler, Daniel, "The Case of the Missing Trade and Other HOV Mysteries," University of Toronto, August 1993, processed.

Vanek, Jaroslav, "The Factor Proportions Theory: The *N*-Factor Case," *Kyklos*, 21 (October 1968), pp. 749-754.

Wood, Adrian, "Give Heckscher and Ohlin a Chance!" *Weltwirtschaftliches Archiv*, 130 (No. 1, 1994a), pp. 20-49.

———, *North-South Trade, Employment and Inequality: Changing Fortunes in a Skill-Driven World*, Oxford, Clarendon, 1994b.

FRANK D. GRAHAM
MEMORIAL LECTURERS

1950–1951	Milton Friedman
1951–1952	James E. Meade
1952–1953	Sir Dennis Robertson
1953–1954	Paul A. Samuelson
1955–1956	Gottfried Haberler
1956–1957	Ragnar Nurkse
1957–1958	Albert O. Hirschman
1959–1960	Robert Triffin
1960–1961	Jacob Viner
1961–1962	Don Patinkin
1962–1963	Friedrich A. Lutz (Essay 41)
1963–1964	Tibor Scitovsky (Essay 49)
1964–1965	Sir John Hicks
1965–1966	Robert A. Mundell
1966–1967	Jagdish N. Bhagwati (Special Paper 8)
1967–1968	Arnold C. Harberger
1968–1969	Harry G. Johnson
1969–1970	Richard N. Cooper (Essay 86)
1970–1971	W. Max Corden (Essay 93)
1971–1972	Richard E. Caves (Special Paper 10)
1972–1973	Paul A. Volcker
1973–1974	J. Marcus Fleming (Essay 107)
1974–1975	Anne O. Krueger (Study 40)
1975–1976	Ronald W. Jones (Special Paper 12)
1976–1977	Ronald I. McKinnon (Essay 125)
1977–1978	Charles P. Kindleberger (Essay 129)
1978–1979	Bertil Ohlin (Essay 134)
1979–1980	Bela Balassa (Essay 141)
1980–1981	Marina von Neumann Whitman (Essay 143)
1981–1982	Robert E. Baldwin (Essay 150)
1983–1984	Stephen Marris (Essay 155)
1984–1985	Rudiger Dornbusch (Essay 165)
1986–1987	Jacob A. Frenkel (Study 63)
1987–1988	Ronald Findlay (Essay 177)
1988–1989	Michael Bruno (Essay 183)
1988–1989	Elhanan Helpman (Special Paper 16)
1989–1990	Michael L. Mussa (Essay 179)
1990-1991	Toyoo Gyohten
1991-1992	Stanley Fischer
1992-1993	Paul Krugman (Essay 190)
1993-1994	Edward E. Leamer (Study 77)

PUBLICATIONS OF THE
INTERNATIONAL FINANCE SECTION

Notice to Contributors

The International Finance Section publishes papers in four series: ESSAYS IN INTERNATIONAL FINANCE, PRINCETON STUDIES IN INTERNATIONAL FINANCE, and SPECIAL PAPERS IN INTERNATIONAL ECONOMICS contain new work not published elsewhere. REPRINTS IN INTERNATIONAL FINANCE reproduce journal articles previously published by Princeton faculty members associated with the Section. The Section welcomes the submission of manuscripts for publication under the following guidelines:

ESSAYS are meant to disseminate new views about international financial matters and should be accessible to well-informed nonspecialists as well as to professional economists. Technical terms, tables, and charts should be used sparingly; mathematics should be avoided.

STUDIES are devoted to new research on international finance, with preference given to empirical work. They should be comparable in originality and technical proficiency to papers published in leading economic journals. They should be of medium length, longer than a journal article but shorter than a book.

SPECIAL PAPERS are surveys of research on particular topics and should be suitable for use in undergraduate courses. They may be concerned with international trade as well as international finance. They should also be of medium length.

Manuscripts should be submitted in triplicate, typed single sided and double spaced throughout on 8½ by 11 white bond paper. Publication can be expedited if manuscripts are computer keyboarded in WordPerfect 5.1 or a compatible program. Additional instructions and a style guide are available from the Section.

How to Obtain Publications

The Section's publications are distributed free of charge to college, university, and public libraries and to nongovernmental, nonprofit research institutions. Eligible institutions may ask to be placed on the Section's permanent mailing list.

Individuals and institutions not qualifying for free distribution may receive all publications for the calendar year for a subscription fee of $40.00. Late subscribers will receive all back issues for the year during which they subscribe. Subscribers should notify the Section promptly of any change in address, giving the old address as well as the new.

Publications may be ordered individually, with payment made in advance. ESSAYS and REPRINTS cost $8.00 each; STUDIES and SPECIAL PAPERS cost $11.00. An additional $1.25 should be sent for postage and handling within the United States, Canada, and Mexico; $1.50 should be added for surface delivery outside the region.

All payments must be made in U.S. dollars. Subscription fees and charges for single issues will be waived for organizations and individuals in countries where foreign-exchange regulations prohibit dollar payments.

Please address all correspondence, submissions, and orders to:

International Finance Section
Department of Economics, Fisher Hall
Princeton University
Princeton, New Jersey 08544-1021

List of Recent Publications

A complete list of publications may be obtained from the International Finance Section.

ESSAYS IN INTERNATIONAL FINANCE

160. Stanley W. Black, *Learning from Adversity: Policy Responses to Two Oil Shocks.* (December 1985)
161. Alexis Rieffel, *The Role of the Paris Club in Managing Debt Problems.* (December 1985)
162. Stephen E. Haynes, Michael M. Hutchison, and Raymond F. Mikesell, *Japanese Financial Policies and the U.S. Trade Deficit.* (April 1986)
163. Arminio Fraga, *German Reparations and Brazilian Debt: A Comparative Study.* (July 1986)
164. Jack M. Guttentag and Richard J. Herring, *Disaster Myopia in International Banking.* (September 1986)
165. Rudiger Dornbusch, *Inflation, Exchange Rates, and Stabilization.* (October 1986)
166. John Spraos, *IMF Conditionality: Ineffectual, Inefficient, Mistargeted.* (December 1986)
167. Rainer Stefano Masera, *An Increasing Role for the ECU: A Character in Search of a Script.* (June 1987)
168. Paul Mosley, *Conditionality as Bargaining Process: Structural-Adjustment Lending, 1980-86.* (October 1987)
169. Paul A. Volcker, Ralph C. Bryant, Leonhard Gleske, Gottfried Haberler, Alexandre Lamfalussy, Shijuro Ogata, Jesús Silva-Herzog, Ross M. Starr, James Tobin, and Robert Triffin, *International Monetary Cooperation: Essays in Honor of Henry C. Wallich.* (December 1987)
170. Shafiqul Islam, *The Dollar and the Policy-Performance-Confidence Mix.* (July 1988)
171. James M. Boughton, *The Monetary Approach to Exchange Rates: What Now Remains?* (October 1988)
172. Jack M. Guttentag and Richard M. Herring, *Accounting for Losses On Sovereign Debt: Implications for New Lending.* (May 1989)
173. Benjamin J. Cohen, *Developing-Country Debt: A Middle Way.* (May 1989)
174. Jeffrey D. Sachs, *New Approaches to the Latin American Debt Crisis.* (July 1989)
175. C. David Finch, *The IMF: The Record and the Prospect.* (September 1989)
176. Graham Bird, *Loan-Loss Provisions and Third-World Debt.* (November 1989)
177. Ronald Findlay, *The "Triangular Trade" and the Atlantic Economy of the Eighteenth Century: A Simple General-Equilibrium Model.* (March 1990)
178. Alberto Giovannini, *The Transition to European Monetary Union.* (November 1990)
179. Michael L. Mussa, *Exchange Rates in Theory and in Reality.* (December 1990)
180. Warren L. Coats, Jr., Reinhard W. Furstenberg, and Peter Isard, *The SDR System and the Issue of Resource Transfers.* (December 1990)

181. George S. Tavlas, *On the International Use of Currencies: The Case of the Deutsche Mark.* (March 1991)
182. Tommaso Padoa-Schioppa, ed., with Michael Emerson, Kumiharu Shigehara, and Richard Portes, *Europe After 1992: Three Essays.* (May 1991)
183. Michael Bruno, *High Inflation and the Nominal Anchors of an Open Economy.* (June 1991)
184. Jacques J. Polak, *The Changing Nature of IMF Conditionality.* (September 1991)
185. Ethan B. Kapstein, *Supervising International Banks: Origins and Implications of the Basle Accord.* (December 1991)
186. Alessandro Giustiniani, Francesco Papadia, and Daniela Porciani, *Growth and Catch-Up in Central and Eastern Europe: Macroeconomic Effects on Western Countries.* (April 1992)
187. Michele Fratianni, Jürgen von Hagen, and Christopher Waller, *The Maastricht Way to EMU.* (June 1992)
188. Pierre-Richard Agénor, *Parallel Currency Markets in Developing Countries: Theory, Evidence, and Policy Implications.* (November 1992)
189. Beatriz Armendariz de Aghion and John Williamson, *The G-7's Joint-and-Several Blunder.* (April 1993)
190. Paul Krugman, *What Do We Need to Know About the International Monetary System?* (July 1993)
191. Peter M. Garber and Michael G. Spencer, *The Dissolution of the Austro-Hungarian Empire: Lessons for Currency Reform.* (February 1994)
192. Raymond F. Mikesell, *The Bretton Woods Debates: A Memoir.* (March 1994)
193. Graham Bird, *Economic Assistance to Low-Income Countries: Should the Link be Resurrected?* (July 1994)
194. Lorenzo Bini-Smaghi, Tommaso Padoa-Schioppa, and Francesco Papadia, *The Transition to EMU in the Maastricht Treaty.* (November 1994)
195. Ariel Buira, *Reflections on the International Monetary System.* (January 1995)

PRINCETON STUDIES IN INTERNATIONAL FINANCE

57. Stephen S. Golub, *The Current-Account Balance and the Dollar: 1977-78 and 1983-84.* (October 1986)
58. John T. Cuddington, *Capital Flight: Estimates, Issues, and Explanations.* (December 1986)
59. Vincent P. Crawford, *International Lending, Long-Term Credit Relationships, and Dynamic Contract Theory.* (March 1987)
60. Thorvaldur Gylfason, *Credit Policy and Economic Activity in Developing Countries with IMF Stabilization Programs.* (August 1987)
61. Stephen A. Schuker, *American "Reparations" to Germany, 1919-33: Implications for the Third-World Debt Crisis.* (July 1988)
62. Steven B. Kamin, *Devaluation, External Balance, and Macroeconomic Performance: A Look at the Numbers.* (August 1988)
63. Jacob A. Frenkel and Assaf Razin, *Spending, Taxes, and Deficits: International-Intertemporal Approach.* (December 1988)
64. Jeffrey A. Frankel, *Obstacles to International Macroeconomic Policy Coordination.* (December 1988)

65. Peter Hooper and Catherine L. Mann, *The Emergence and Persistence of the U.S. External Imbalance, 1980-87.* (October 1989)

66. Helmut Reisen, *Public Debt, External Competitiveness, and Fiscal Discipline in Developing Countries.* (November 1989)

67. Victor Argy, Warwick McKibbin, and Eric Siegloff, *Exchange-Rate Regimes for a Small Economy in a Multi-Country World.* (December 1989)

68. Mark Gersovitz and Christina H. Paxson, *The Economies of Africa and the Prices of Their Exports.* (October 1990)

69. Felipe Larraín and Andrés Velasco, *Can Swaps Solve the Debt Crisis? Lessons from the Chilean Experience.* (November 1990)

70. Kaushik Basu, *The International Debt Problem, Credit Rationing and Loan Pushing: Theory and Experience.* (October 1991)

71. Daniel Gros and Alfred Steinherr, *Economic Reform in the Soviet Union: Pas de Deux between Disintegration and Macroeconomic Destabilization.* (November 1991)

72. George M. von Furstenberg and Joseph P. Daniels, *Economic Summit Declarations, 1975-1989: Examining the Written Record of International Cooperation.* (February 1992)

73. Ishac Diwan and Dani Rodrik, *External Debt, Adjustment, and Burden Sharing: A Unified Framework.* (November 1992)

74. Barry Eichengreen, *Should the Maastricht Treaty Be Saved?* (December 1992)

75. Adam Klug, *The German Buybacks, 1932-1939: A Cure for Overhang?* (November 1993)

76. Tamim Bayoumi and Barry Eichengreen, *One Money or Many? Analyzing the Prospects for Monetary Unification in Various Parts of the World.* (September 1994)

77. Edward E. Leamer, *The Heckscher-Ohlin Model in Theory and Practice.* (February 1995)

SPECIAL PAPERS IN INTERNATIONAL ECONOMICS

16. Elhanan Helpman, *Monopolistic Competition in Trade Theory.* (June 1990)

17. Richard Pomfret, *International Trade Policy with Imperfect Competition.* (August 1992)

18. Hali J. Edison, *The Effectiveness of Central-Bank Intervention: A Survey of the Literature After 1982.* (July 1993)

REPRINTS IN INTERNATIONAL FINANCE

26. Peter B. Kenen, *The Use of IMF Credit*; reprinted from *Pulling Together: The International Monetary Fund in a Multipolar World*, 1989. (December 1989)

27. Peter B. Kenen, *Transitional Arrangements for Trade and Payments Among the CMEA Countries*; reprinted from *International Monetary Fund Staff Papers* 38 (2), 1991. (July 1991)

28. Peter B. Kenen, *Ways to Reform Exchange-Rate Arrangements*; reprinted from *Bretton Woods: Looking to the Future*, 1994. (November 1994)